CHESTER NEZ
AND THE
UNBREAKABLE CODE
A NAVAJO CODE TALKER'S STORY

JOSEPH BRUCHAC

ILLUSTRATED BY
LIZ AMINI-HOLMES

ALBERT WHITMAN & COMPANY
CHICAGO, ILLINOIS

ACKNOWLEDGMENTS

Thanks to those Navajo friends and fellow writers such as Nia Francisco, Laura Tohe, Rex Lee Jim, Luci Tapahonso, Shonto Begay, and Harry Walters who have, over the years, helped me gain some understanding of the complex and inspiring culture and history of the Dineh people. Thanks to the Navajo Code Talkers Association and the code talkers I've met, in particular Keith Little, Samuel Smith, and Samuel Holiday, whose book about his own experiences in World War II, *Under the Eagle*, should be on everyone's must-read list. And, lastly, very special thanks to Mike Nez, Chester's son, for his feedback, to Latham Nez, Chester's grandson, and to Judith Avila for so generously advising us on this book and for having helped Chester Nez tell his story in *Code Talker: The First and Only Memoir by One of the Original Navajo Code Talkers of WWII*.

To my wife and constant inspiration: Nicola Marae Allain—JB
To my family that encircles me with love and support—LA-H

Library of Congress Cataloging-in-Publication data is on file with the publisher.

Text copyright © 2018 by Joseph Bruchac
Illustrations copyright © 2018 by Liz Amini-Holmes
First published in the United States of America in 2018 by Albert Whitman & Company
ISBN 978-0-8075-0007-1 (hardcover)
ISBN 978-0-8075-0008-8 (ebook)

Printed in the United States of America
10 9 8 7 6 5 4 LB 24 23 22 21 20 19

Design by Ellen Kokontis

For more information about Albert Whitman & Company,
visit our website at www.albertwhitman.com.

OCTOBER 1929: MONTH OF SMALL WIND

When Betoli was eight years old, the time came for him to go to boarding school. He had to leave his family, his home, and the goats and sheep he loved and took care of.

He climbed into the back of the missionary's truck.

"You need an English name," the missionary said. Betoli's name was Navajo, like he was.

"You will be Chester," the man said.

At Fort Defiance School, the matrons shaved off
Chester's long hair and gave him a blue uniform to wear.
They made him use English, a language
he'd never spoken, and when Chester spoke
Navajo, the matrons washed out his mouth
with yellow soap.

"Navajo is bad! Speak only English!"

Many years earlier, in the 1860s, the US Army had held Navajos captive at Fort Defiance. From there, the army forced the Navajos to go on the Long Walk, a journey of 300 miles into what is now New Mexico. Many people suffered and died.

Fort Defiance was now a boarding school for Navajo children. But some of the youngest students had bad dreams because of the fort's history. Chester did his best to calm their fears at night. He reminded them they were not alone. They still had families back home.

JUNE 1932: MONTH OF BIG PLANTING

Over the summer, Chester returned home, where he could again speak the sacred language the Holy People had given the Navajos long ago. When he cared for the sheep and goats and prayed using corn pollen, he felt like a real Navajo, living the Right Way.

His heart was strong again. Being home took away the loneliness Chester felt at school.

SEPTEMBER 1932: MONTH OF HALF

Chester returned to school, where he was again told his Navajo language was worthless.

"You must use only English to survive in the white man's world!" the matrons said.

Chester knew he might need to live in the white man's world one day. In that world speaking English was essential, so he worked hard and did well. Chester enjoyed learning and wanted to prove his worth. He also learned to pray the Catholic way and served as an altar boy.

The Catholic way was good, but so was the Navajo way.

Though he spoke English in school, Chester kept his love for his Navajo people and their language. He decided to never break the ties that bound him to them.

DECEMBER 1941: MONTH OF CRUSTED SNOW

Chester was in tenth grade when the school principal called the students together.

"The Japanese Empire attacked us at Pearl Harbor," he said. "We are at war."

The United States had fought the Navajos years ago, but now the United States was their country too. Chester thought about how his ancestors stood up against enemies. He should act with the same courage. Protecting his homeland was an honor.

"I am a warrior," Chester said to himself. "I will fight for this land."

APRIL 1942: MONTH OF BIG PLANT

Recruiters from the US Marines Corps came to the Reservation. "We need Navajo men who speak English and Navajo," they said.

The US military needed a new way to send its secret messages. The messages were sent in code over the radio, but since anyone's radio could receive those messages, the enemy could hear them too. The Japanese had broken every American code. The marines tried using a coding machine, the Shackle, to create an unbreakable code, but the machine took too long to encode and decode messages.

Then a former army soldier, a missionary's son who had once lived on the Navajo reservation, suggested using Navajo, a language almost impossible for non-Navajos to speak.

The marines agreed to try it.

Many Navajos volunteered to join the marines, but only twenty-nine were chosen, including Chester. They became Platoon 382.

Suddenly the language he had been told to forget was important. Chester was proud he had never given up speaking Navajo.

JUNE 1942: MONTH OF BIG PLANTING

After basic training, Platoon 382 went to Camp Elliott near San Diego. An officer took the platoon into a room. "Create an unbreakable code," he told them. "Start by choosing one word for every letter of the English alphabet."

Then the officer left, locking the twenty-nine men in that room.

Chester wondered how they would begin.

Then one of the men, Gene Crawford, spoke up. He knew how military codes worked. "Make every word clear and different from every other," he said to the others.

They used English words for each letter of the alphabet. *A* was *ant.*
B was *bear. C* was *cat.* Then they chose the Navajo words for each of
those English words. *Ant* was *Wol-la-chee. Bear* was *Shush.* Cat was *Moasi.*

By the end of the first day, they had the whole alphabet.

A few weeks later, three more Navajo men joined the team.
Now thirty-two soldiers were creating the code and learning to use it.

Instead of spelling out some items in the English alphabet, they
chose Navajo words to represent them. *Battleship* became *lo-tso,* which
means "whale." *Bombs* were *a-ye-shi,* or "eggs." There was a lot to
remember, but Chester enjoyed what they were doing and had an
excellent memory.

SEPTEMBER 1942: MONTH OF HALF

After thirteen weeks, Platoon 382 demonstrated their code to marine officials.

Expert code breakers could not break it. The code was strong.

The code was efficient too. The Shackle code machine took four hours to encrypt and decrypt a message Navajos could send and receive in less than three minutes. The Navajo language solved the marines' communications problem.

The military ordered the platoon to keep the code a secret.
Only commanders and officers knew about the Navajo code.
Two men stayed behind to teach new Navajo recruits while
Chester and the rest of the code talkers shipped out to the Pacific.
The time had come to use the code in battle.

When their boat reached the island of Guadalcanal, Chester and his partner Roy Begay waded ashore. They dug a foxhole in the sand, and then they were ready. When a runner handed them their first message, they radioed it to two code talkers on the ship offshore.

"Beh-na-ali-tsosie (enemy) a-knah-as-donih ah-toh (machine gun nest) nish-na-jih-goh dah-di-kad (on your right flank). Ah-deel-tahi (Destroy)."

Minutes after their message was received, artillery fire hit the machine gun nest. Chester shouted, "You see that?" Their Navajo code was working!

Chester and the other code talkers sent messages on Guadalcanal for many months, until the Japanese were defeated. Then they were sent to other islands in the Pacific.

The soldiers saw terrible things in combat. They dodged artillery fire, witnessed explosions, and watched men die. Chester was worn out and ill but kept working.

Every day he prayed in Navajo, using corn pollen from his medicine bag. The Navajo way gave him strength and helped him survive until he could go home.

JANUARY 1945: MONTH OF SMALL EAGLE

Chester was finally home.

But he'd seen too much death. He felt at times as if he were dead too.

Chester could not tell anyone, not even his family, about the Navajo code. It was still a secret.

Keeping that secret brought back the loneliness that hurt so much when he first went to school.

Chester's family knew he needed help. They arranged an Enemy Way, a four-day-long ceremony to help someone exposed to the evil of war.

This ceremony was also done for children returning from boarding schools like Fort Defiance. Chester knew that being at school, with its military structure and harsh discipline, was similar to enduring war.

The ceremony restored Chester to the trail of beauty and the
Right Way. He no longer dreamed of war.

SEPTEMBER 1945: MONTH OF HALF

Eight months after Chester came home, the Japanese surrendered and the war was over. The Navajo code had been vital to the war effort. Code talkers had served with every marine unit.

By the end of the war, more than 400 Navajos had served as code talkers. They had been told in school that their language was no good, but they had proven that wasn't true.

The Navajo code helped win World War II.

Like his people who survived the Long Walk, Chester had never forgotten his Navajo heritage.

Despite being told to give up his Navajo language and culture, he found ways to merge them with the white man's world.

His spirit stayed unbroken.

He kept his feet on the trail of beauty.

AUTHOR'S NOTE

Chester Nez went on to serve stateside in the Korean War, from which he was discharged as a corporal. Chester also continued his schooling at the University of Kansas from 1946 to 1952, where he studied commercial art. He married, had children, and gained a reputation as an artist without telling anyone about his role as a code talker.

Years passed and still Chester and the other Navajo code talkers kept their secret.

Finally in 1968, the military decided that with new technology, the Navajo code was no longer needed. The code was declassified, and their secret was released after twenty-nine years.

In 1982, President Ronald Reagan declared August 14 National Code Talkers Day, and more people began to learn their story. In December 2000, President Bill Clinton signed into law an act honoring the code talkers. The original twenty-nine were given gold medals, and all the code talkers who followed were given silver ones.

Chester appreciated being invited to the White House and being given those honors. But what he felt best about was that he had been able to live the Right Way as a Navajo, holding on to his language and traditions despite being told in school to give up his culture.

Eventually, with the help of Judith Avila, Chester decided to tell his story. It was published in 2011 as the book *Code Talker: The First and Only Memoir by One of the Original Navajo Code Talkers of WWII.*

Chester was the last survivor of the twenty-nine original Navajo recruits who created the unbreakable code. He passed away on June 4, 2014, at the age of ninety-three at his home in Albuquerque, New Mexico. Chester's name and that of hundreds of other Navajo men who served as code talkers in World War II can be seen on the bricks of the Veterans' Memorial in Window Rock, Arizona, in the heart of the enduring Navajo Nation.

THE NAVAJO CODE

(A portion of the code from the Naval History and Heritage Command)

ALPHABET	NAVAJO WORD	LITERAL TRANSLATION
A	WOL-LA-CHEE	Ant
B	SHUSH	Bear
C	MOASI	Cat
D	LHA-CHA-EH	Dog
E	AH-JAH	Ear
F	MA-E	Fox
G	AH-TAD	Girl
H	TSE-GAH	Hair
I	TKIN	Ice
J	AH-YA-TSINNE	Jaw
K	KLIZZIE-YAZZIE	Kid
L	AH-JAD	Leg
M	NA-AS-TSO-SI	Mouse
N	A-CHIN	Nose
O	NE-AHS-JAH	Owl
P	CLA-GI-AIH	Pant
Q	CA-YEILTH	Quiver
R	GAH	Rabbit
S	DIBEH	Sheep
T	D-AH	Tea
U	SHI-DA	Uncle
V	A-KEH-DI-GLINI	Victor
W	GLOE-IH	Weasel

X	AL-NA-AS-DZOH	Cross
Y	TSAH-AS-ZIH	Yucca
Z	BESH-DO-TLIZ	Zinc

Battleship	LO-TSO	Whale
Bomb	A-YE-SHI	Eggs
Craft	AH-TOH	Nest
Cruiser	LO-TSO-YAZZIE	Small Whale
Demolition	AH-DEEL-TAHI	Blow Up
Destroyer	CA-LO	Shark
Flank	DAH-DI-KAD	Flank
Grenade	NI-MA-SI	Potatoes
Machine Gun	A-KNAH-AS-DONIH	Rapid-Fire Gun
Submarine	BESH-LO	Iron Fish

January	ATSAH-BE-YAZ	Small Eagle
February	WOZ-CHEIND	Squeaky Voice
March	TAH-CHILL	Small Plant
April	TAH-TSO	Big Plant
May	TAH-TSOSIE	Small Plant
June	BE-NE-EH-EH-JAH-TSO	Big Planting
July	BE-NE-TA-TSOSIE	Small Harvest
August	BE-NEEN-TA-TSO	Big Harvest
September	GHAW-JIH	Half
October	NIL-CHI-TSOSIE	Small Wind
November	NIL-CHI-TSO	Big Wind
December	YAS-NIL-TES	Crusted Snow

TIMELINE

1921 Born January 23 in New Mexico

1929 Sent to boarding school at Fort Defiance, Arizona

1942 Enlists in the Marine Corps

1945 World War II ends; Chester leaves active duty and becomes part of the Marine Reserves

1946 Attends the University of Kansas to study commercial arts

1951 Called to active duty for Korean War

1952 Discontinues studies at the University of Kansas when his GI bill runs out

1968 Navajo code declassified

1974 Retires from working as a painter at the Raymond G. Murphy Veterans Affairs Medical Center

1982 President Ronald Reagan proclaims August 14 Navajo Code Talkers Day

2000 Legislation to honor Navajo Code Talkers passes Congress and is signed by President Bill Clinton on December 21

2001 Original twenty-nine Navajo Code Talkers receive the Congressional Gold Medal of Honor from President George W. Bush

2011 Writes memoir, *Code Talker: The First and Only Memoir by One of the Original Navajo Code Talkers of WWII*, with Judith Avila

2012 Awarded honorary degree from the University of Kansas

2014 Chester Nez dies at the age of ninety-three on June 4